WELCOME TO
EVERGLADES
NATIONAL PARK

BY NADIA HIGGINS

Many thanks to the staff at Everglades National Park for their assistance with this book.

MAP KEY
The maps throughout this
book use the following icons:

 Alligator or Crocodile
Viewing Area

 Birds

 Campground

Driving Excursion

Hiking Trail

Visitor Center

Manatee Viewing Area

Picnic Area

 Point of Interest

Ranger Station

Lodging

About National Parks

A national park is an area of land that has been set aside by Congress. National parks protect nature and history. In most cases, no hunting, grazing, or farming is allowed. The first national park in the United States—and in the world—was Yellowstone National Park. It is located in parts of Wyoming, Idaho, and Montana. It was founded in 1872. In 1916, the U.S. National Park Service began.

Today, the National Park Service manages more than 380 sites. Some of these sites are historic, such as the Statue of Liberty or Martin Luther King, Jr. National Historic Site. Other park areas preserve wild land. The National Park Service manages 40% of the nation's wilderness areas, including national parks. Each year, millions of people from around the world visit these national parks. Visitors may camp, go canoeing, or go for a hike. Or, they may simply sit and enjoy the scenery, wildlife, and the quiet of the land.

TABLE OF

The Child's World®

**Published in the
United States of America
by The Child's World®**

PO Box 326
Chanhassen, MN 55317-0326
800-599-READ
www.childsworld.com

Acknowledgements
The Child's World®: Mary Berendes,
Publishing Director

Content Consultant: Laura Law, Former Hidden Lake
Supervisory Park Ranger, Everglades National Park

The Design Lab: Kathleen Petelinsek,
Design and Page Production

Map Hero, Inc.: Matt Kania, Cartographer

Red Line Editorial: Bob Temple, Editorial Direction

Photo Credits
Cover and this page: M. Botzek/zefa/Corbis

Interior: Bettman/Corbis: 14; blickwinkel/Alamy:
20 (right); Corbis: 15; Daniel J. Cox/Corbis: 25;
David Muench/Corbis: 18–19; Galen Rowell/
Corbis: 10–11, 23 (left); George McCarthy/Corbis:
26–27; Jeff Greenberg/PhotoEdit, Inc.: 13; Jim
Richardson/Corbis: 16; Kevin Schafer/Corbis: 20
(left); Richard Hamilton Smith/Corbis: 2–3; Stan
Osolinski/Corbis: 6–7; Wayne Bennett /Corbis: 23
(right); W. Perry Conway/Corbis: 8–9; Yann Arthus-
Bertrand/Corbis: 1.

**Library of Congress
Cataloging-in-Publication Data**
Higgins, Nadia.
  Welcome to Everglades National Park /
by Nadia Higgins.
     p. cm. — (Visitor guides)
  Includes index.
  ISBN 1-59296-702-7 (library bound : alk.
paper)
  1. Everglades National Park (Fla.)—Juvenile
literature. I. Title. II. Series.
  F317.E9H54 2006
  917.59'3902—dc22   2005030075

On the cover and this page
A young American alligator rests
amongst water plants on a late
afternoon.

On page 1
From the air, the islands and plants
of Everglades National Park look like
crazy puzzle pieces.

On pages 2–3
Mangrove trees like this one are
very important in the Everglades.
They live in water that is a mixture of
saltwater and freshwater, and their
roots help protect the land from high
winds and waves.

WELCOME TO EVERGLADES NATIONAL PARK

Λ

CONTENTS

A Web of Life

Welcome to Everglades National Park! You have arrived at one of the largest wilderness areas in the United States. It is also one of the world's most important **wetlands**. Here, on the southern tip of Florida, is a land of soggy **marshes** and waist-deep ponds. Tree islands and forests rise out of the flat, water-soaked land.

An amazing number of plants and animals live here. Some, such as the Florida panther, are found only in south Florida. They are almost never seen. Many alligators live in the muddy waters. Birds nest in thick tangles of trees. Fish feed on newly hatched mosquitoes.

FLORIDA

Everglades National Park

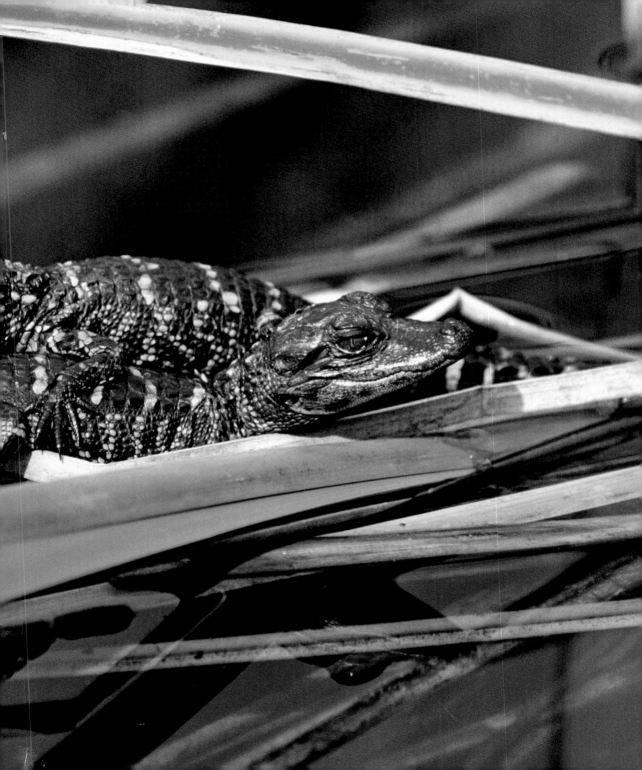

The plants and animals depend on each other and the land to survive. They live together as part of an **ecosystem**, or web of life. Everglades National Park was created to protect this ecosystem.

Human Food

When a mosquito bites you here, you become part of the Everglades' **food chain**. You provide food for the mosquito. In turn, the mosquito is eaten by a tree frog, fish, lizard, or snake. Then these animals are food for even bigger ones such as wading birds and alligators.

Two Seasons

This area of Florida is usually warm or hot all year long. It has just two seasons—a wet season and a dry season. The best time to visit the park is during the dry season. This is from December through April. Temperatures are comfortable and there aren't as many mosquitoes. You also don't have to worry as much about an afternoon thunderstorm.

It's also easier to see animals during the dry season. As the rains die down, swamps turn into hard, dry land. The areas of water get smaller. Since animals depend on the water to survive, they gather in high numbers near the wet areas. When it rains again, the land floods. The animals spread out over the park again.

Gator Holes

Alligators clean plants and muck out of holes in the ground. This makes the holes larger, and they fill with water. During the dry season, these water holes are the only home for large numbers of fish, frogs, snails, and other animals. The alligators then feast on their visitors.

These two alligators are spending a lazy afternoon resting in a gator hole. American alligators were once so rare, they became **endangered** in 1967. Today, the number of alligators has grown, and these animals are slowly making a comeback. American alligators can be found in Florida, Georgia, Texas, Louisiana, and North and South Carolina.

A Troubled Past

A good place to start your trip is the Ernest F. Coe Visitor Center. Here you can buy I.D. cards of birds and plants with pictures on them. The cards will help you spot the birds and plants when you go on hikes.

You can also learn facts about the history of the park. In the late 1920s and until the '40s, Ernest F. Coe fought to make the land a national park. Many others viewed the area as a worthless swamp. People were draining the soil to make way for farms and cities. The Everglades area was drying up. As the ecosystem became unbalanced, plants and animals began to die.

The Ernest F. Coe Visitor Center has many places, like this gazebo, for people to watch nearby plants and animals. The center also has numerous exhibits and maps for visitors to learn more about the park.

👫 This picture, taken in 1945, shows two Seminole people as they paddled down Tamiami Trail toward their village.

👫 Opposite page: A group of Seminole people in traditional dress as they stood outside their hut in 1926.

Everglades Hideaway

In the mid-1800s, the government tried to force Native Americans in the southeast to leave their homes and move west. Some Miccosukee and Seminole Indians refused to go. Groups of them escaped to the Everglades. Life wasn't easy in this swampy wilderness. Still, they lived in harmony with the land for many years. Seminole and Miccosukee Native Americans live near Everglades National Park, even today.

In 1947, the park officially opened. However, much damage to the water supply had already been done—and still continues today. The wetlands of southern Florida are less than half the size they were 100 years ago. The area has just one-tenth the number of birds that it had 200 years ago.

In fact, Everglades National Park is one of the most threatened of all the national parks. Today, lawmakers, scientists, and many others are carrying out a plan to save the land. Much work still needs to be done, however.

The waters of the Everglades' **sloughs** may look like they are still, but they are actually moving—about 100 feet (30 m) per day.

A River of Grass

Head for the Anhinga Trail. The trail is named after one of the many kinds of birds that can be spotted here. It is about a half-mile (1 km) long.

This trail is a wooden boardwalk that takes you around a slough (pronounced "slew"). A slough is a waterway running through the wetland. Sloughs are usually just a few feet deep, but they are the deepest areas of water in the park.

Here you'll discover why the Everglades is called a "river of grass." Fields of gently swaying sawgrass grow along the edges of the slough. Watch out, though! Blades of sawgrass are sharp enough to cut your skin.

Look toward the base of the sawgrass. You may see the white egg sacs of apple snails. The eggs will hatch in just a few weeks. The snails will be food for one of the Everglades' most famous birds—the snail kite. The bird's hooked beak is just right for pulling the snail from its shell.

You may notice that some of the sawgrass is moving. There's a good chance an alligator is moving below. Make sure you stay well back. If the alligator hisses or opens its mouth, back away even more. You'll still be able to see its bumpy back sticking out of the water.

Sawgrass is not actually a grass at all—it's a plant called a *sedge*. Sawgrass can grow to be up to 10 feet (3 m) high, and each one of its blades can be up to 3 feet (1 m) long.

🚶🚶 Above: Gumbo limbo trees are known for their red, flaky bark. These trees grow quickly and often stand about 40 feet (12 m) high.

🚶🚶 Right: From close up you can see how the roots of a strangler fig seem to be "strangling" another tree. In a few years, the fig will take over and

Tree Islands

Your next hike is the nearby Gumbo Limbo Trail. This trail takes you to one of the many small islands that rise out of the river of grass. The islands, called hardwood **hammocks**, are like small jungles. Lush, green trees and plants cover the land.

As the name suggests, you'll see gumbo limbo trees on this shady trail. Notice the red bark. It's normal for the bark to be peeling off.

Do you see brown roots wrapping around a gumbo limbo tree? Those roots belong to another tree, the strangler fig. Strangler figs kill other trees. This strangler fig will eventually "strangle" the gumbo limbo tree and take its place in the forest.

Pinelands

The next trail, the Pineland Trail, takes you to a pine tree forest. Sunlight shines through the tops of slash pine trees. Listen for the drumming of a woodpecker. Look for lizards and snakes. If you're lucky, you may even see a Florida wild turkey.

All of Everglades National Park is on low land, right around sea level. However, just a few feet in elevation make a big difference. Lower lands, like the slough at Anhinga Trail, are the wettest. They are flooded longest during the wet season. The pinelands are on higher ground. That means this is drier land. Wildfires sparked by lightning spread easily across this drier land.

You may see that some of the trees are black on one side. They have been burned by fire. Fire is actually good for the pine trees. Their thick bark protects them from burning down. However, the fire *does* destroy other types of trees that grow here. These trees grow faster than pine trees. They can block out sunlight that young pine trees need to grow. Fire protects pine trees by

killing these competing trees. In fact, if fire doesn't happen naturally, the park service may start one on purpose.

Tall slash pine trees and spiky palmetto plants are even more beautiful

Florida Panther

The Florida panther is one of the most endangered animals in North America. Only 30 to 50 of the panthers are left in the wild. A few live in the pinelands of the Everglades. The biggest threat to this animal is that the land it lives on is being destroyed. Much of the panther's **habitat** has been destroyed by development

By the Ocean

Now head south toward the Atlantic Ocean. Take a walk around Florida Bay. There's a good chance you'll spot a manatee. Manatees are nicknamed "gentle sea cows." These **mammals** are actually close relatives of the elephant.

You may notice that some manatees have scars on their backs. That's from getting run over by motorboats. Boating accidents are a big threat to manatees. For this reason, park signs tell boaters to turn off their engines when they approach waters where manatees might be swimming.

At the Flamingo Visitor Center, sign up for a ranger-led canoe trip. The tour will take you through the mangrove forests that line the coast. Like all the plants and animals at the Everglades, mangrove trees have special features that help them survive here. Their leathery leaves stand up to the harsh sun. Their stilt-like roots grow right out of the water.

Most adult manatees are about 12 feet (4 m) long and weigh about 1,000 pounds (454 kg). Manatees move very slowly and spend most of the day eating and sleeping. Manatees eat only water plants and can eat up to 150 pounds (68 kg) in one day.

American crocodiles like this one are endangered; fewer than 1,200 remain in the wild. Adults can grow to be 15 feet (5 m) long and weigh up to 450 pounds (204 kg). What's the easiest way to tell the difference between an American crocodile and an American alligator? Look at their snouts! American crocodiles have long, skinny snouts, and their bottom teeth can be seen when their mouths are closed. American alligators have much rounder, wider snouts—see page 4 for a picture of an American alligator.

The water that mangroves grow in is a mix of salty water from the ocean and fresh water from the wetland. The salt water would kill most other types of trees, so mangroves grow by themselves here.

Now is your only chance to spot a crocodile. Alligators live in many areas of the Everglades, but crocodiles don't go very far away from the mangrove wilderness.

The Everglades is the only area in the world where alligators and crocodiles live side by side. However, alligators outnumber their shy cousins by about 500 to one. Crocodiles are one of the 15 endangered species protected by the park.

Your visit to Everglades National Park is almost over. As darkness falls, listen to the night sounds. Hear the hoot of a barred owl. Listen for frogs croaking, and the hum of crickets. These sounds tell the story of a wilderness like none other on Earth.

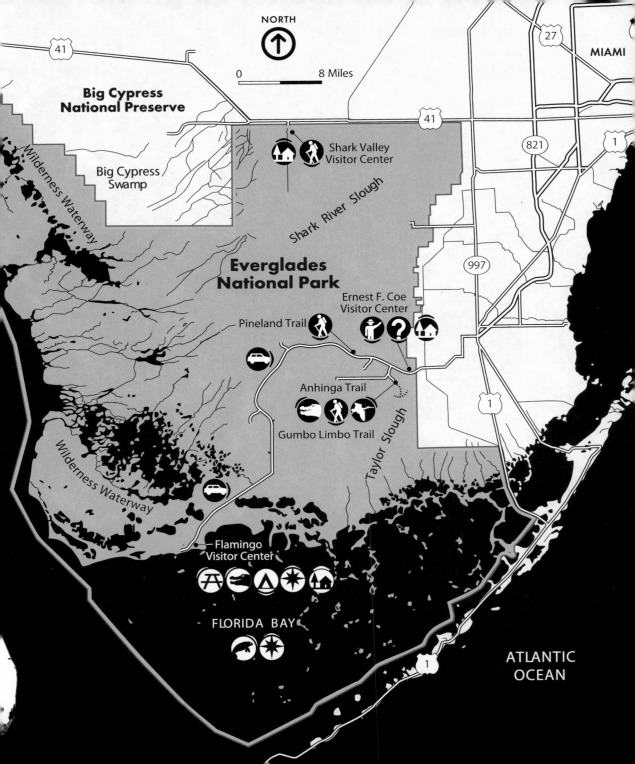

NORTH

0   8 Miles

41

Big Cypress National Preserve

Big Cypress Swamp

Wilderness Waterway

Shark Valley Visitor Center

Shark River Slough

41

27

MIAMI

821

1

997

Everglades National Park

Ernest F. Coe Visitor Center

Pineland Trail

Anhinga Trail

Gumbo Limbo Trail

Taylor Slough

Wilderness Waterway

1

Flamingo Visitor Center

FLORIDA BAY

1

ATLANTIC OCEAN

EVERGLADES NATIONAL PARK FAST FACTS

Date opened: December 6, 1947

Location: Southern Florida

Size: More than 2,300 square miles/5,957 sq km; about 1.5 million acres/607,028 hectares

Major habitats: Sawgrass prairie, slough, hardwood hammock, mangrove swamp, and pineland

Elevation:
    Highest: 8 feet/2 m
    Lowest: Sea level

Weather:
    Average yearly rainfall: 60 inches/152 cm
    Average temperatures: 87 F/31 C to 53 F/12 C

Number of animal species: More than 350 kinds of birds, 66 reptile and amphibian species, and more than 40 types of mammals

Main animal species: Herons, squirrels, mice, manatees, bobcats, alligators, frogs, and turtles

Number of endangered animal species: 15

Number of plant species: More than 1,000

Main plant species: Sawgrass, mangrove trees, cypress trees, and slash pine trees

Number of endangered plant species: 2

Native people: Tequesta, Calusa, Jeaga, Ais, Mayaimi (gone by 1750); Miccosukee and Seminole (from early 1800s until today)

Number of visitors each year: More than 1.5 million

Important sites and landmarks: Shark River Slough, Taylor Slough, Big Cypress Swamp, and Wilderness Waterway

Tourist activities: Nature walks, boat tours, bird watching, canoeing, and camping

GLOSSARY

ecosystem (EE-koh-sis-tum): A community of plants and animals that rely on each other and the land and weather to survive is called an ecosystem. The Everglades ecosystem depends a lot on water.

endangered (en-DAYN-jurd): When an entire plant or animal species is dying out, it is endangered. American crocodiles are endangered.

food chain (FOOD CHAYN): A food chain is a way of listing a group of animals to show how they feed on each other. An animal in the middle of the list eats the ones below it. In turn, that animal in the middle is eaten by the animal above it. Plants are at the bottom of the food chain.

habitat (HAB-uh-tat): An animal's natural home is its habitat. The wetland is the habitat of alligators.

hammocks (HAM-muks): Small islands that rise slightly out of a swamp are hammocks. Hammocks are covered with trees and plants.

mammals (MAM-mullz): Warm-blooded animals that have a backbone and feed their young on mothers' milk are mammals. Most mammals, such as humans, monkeys, cows, and mice, have hair or fur.

marshes (MARSH-ez): Soft, wet lands that are often flooded are marshes. Trees don't grow in marshes.

sloughs (SLOOZ): The wettest areas of a wetland are sloughs. People can canoe on the sloughs at Everglades National Park.

wetlands (WET-lands): Areas that include swamps, marshes, and sloughs are wetlands. Wetlands are low, flat land.

TO FIND OUT MORE

∧

FURTHER READING

George, Jean Craighead and Wendell Minor (photographer and illustrator).
Everglades.
New York: HarperCollins, 1995.

Marx, Trish and Cindy Karp (photographer).
Everglades Forever: Restoring America's Great Wetland.
New York: Lee & Low Books, 2004.

Stewart, Melissa and Stephen K. Maka (photographer).
Life in a Wetland.
Minneapolis, MN: Lerner Publications, 2003.

ON THE WEB

Visit our home page for lots of links
about Everglades National Park:

http://www.childsworld.com/links

NOTE TO PARENTS, TEACHERS, AND LIBRARIANS:
We routinely check our Web links to make sure
they're safe, active sites—so encourage your
readers to check them out!

INDEX